The Captain of your Life

7 Easy steps to throw away failure, jump start your life and get what you really want.

Gustavo Alberto Hernandez

© Prometheus Griffin Publishing

The Captain of your life

DEDICATION

To my parents. Who always instigated me to never surrender (except if necessary to continue living, re-group and fight again until I win).

To my Wingman and his wife Emily, who yanked me out of my paradigms by example.

To Nhu, who opened my eyes to see I could do this.

Preface:

Dear reader and friend. If you have come to reach for this book is because you want more of your life or want to achieve more; maybe you are looking back and you find you have run your race and find yourself nowhere or are displeased with the results; somehow, somewhere you know inside of you that you can do better. On the other hand or perhaps you have done well, but you think it is time to turn your life and aim to higher and fulfilling things.

The biggest complaint of any person I have met is that they believe they do not have any power to change their life or circumstances. They have tried and for some reason or another they fail to achieve the desired results.

Well, I have great news, and those news

are that you can change your life right here, and right now! Of course you will need to do something, and by purchasing this book you have taken your first step to commence your life overhaul, but now as you read these pages, you can rest assured that altering your course of events is on its way for you. Congratulations!

I was very pleased to write this book, I realize today more than ever there is a great need to change things, people, societies and even governments. Regrettably millions of people are stuck in the wrong paradigm and hence their lives are stagnated, hence a new order of things is necessary.

Well, sit down and relax. Hold on tight because the answers are at hand.

The Captain of your life

CONTENTS

1   Step 1. Challenge your establishment   1

2   Step 2. Control your money   13

3   Step 3. Your Health   35

4   Step 4. Improve your relationships   57

5   Step 5. Take control of your work life   73

6   Step 6. Close the door to your past   95

7   Step 7. Wake up your hidden potential   103

"Newton's First Law of Motion states that a body at rest will remain at rest unless an _outside force_ acts on it, and a body in motion at a constant velocity will remain in motion in a straight line unless acted upon by an _outside force_."

"Knowing others is wisdom, knowing your self is Enlightenment"
- Lao-Tzu

Step 1. Challenge your establishment.

I feel very lucky in my life and I would not change it for anybody else's. Yes, I have had my ups and downs like everyone else, but since I was young I have always kept going looking for more.

I became a teenager during the big 80's, and to me those were fantastic days to be young. I grew up with MTV watching and listening to great groups like Tears for Fears, Level 42, Duran Duran among others.

Back then we did not have cell phones or any known high end electronic devices for that matter, but I had a great life being my friends or just walking home from school. It was a simple life but always full of dreams.

Among my favorite singers back then was Cindy Lauper. I really was not a fan of her attire, but I thought she had a great lively voice. On the other hand I never quite liked Madonna. I guess she was OK, but besides from the show, gestures and contortions she made, I really saw not much talent in her.

I anticipated she was going to come and then go to disappear into anonymity just like many other one song wonders in American music history.

But now you certainly like me know what happened... surprise, surprise, it went the opposite way! Madonna is still a big name (and still looks good) whereas my dear Cindy was gone with the wind. Why? Well, it is very simple, Madonna understood a great principle; the principle that you cannot remain the same all your life, you need to simply adapt to the always changing times, so she learned to reinvent herself; in fact she has reinvented herself many times over since I remember.

A friend of mine told me once this. "I can predict your future" Oh yeah? - I said; go ahead, tell me... and so he did... "If you keep doing what you are doing in the same way you have done it, your next 10 years will be exactly like the past 10 years"

How true that was! How true that is! Just like Newton's first law of motion, all will be the same unless an outside force acts on it.

However, as humans that we are, I can say that all your life will remain the same unless an outside (or inside) force acts upon you. So if you are tired of your life and want to improve it, but you keep doing the same things, guess what? Nothing will change.

I like to study quantum physics. And as you study more and more, it will be inevitable for you to bump into the fact that now it is proclaimed that your thoughts and mind can change or alter matter. There are many publications and there are even physicists that have come with some ideas supporting that train of thought, however, I am a very practical man, but I do believe that it is as they say: "mind over matter", but to me it works like this: _If you do not mind, it doesn't matter_!

So, the opposite way is true as well... _if you mind, then it matters_. Wherever your thoughts are, that is where your attention is. Have you ever stopped and listen to your internal chatter? What are the things that you say to yourself on an everyday basis? What is it that comes out of the people you are around? What is it that you hear in the media you tune in every day?

In reality the principle is very simple. You are what you think, why? Because in all truth **you act** in accordance to your thinking. Whatever is in your head that is what you will do. Change your thinking and you will change your actions. If you change your actions you will change your future! Just like that. If you think life is great, you will go through life with please and ease, confident and assured of yourself because all things work out great for you always. Even if bad things happen the world will not end, you dust yourself off and move on; however, If you think life is unfair and bad, you will go through life in defense mode, suspicious of everything and anyone... and let me tell you, that, I have experienced, and I can tell you as well that regrettably, your attitude will permeate to everything you are and do; people and circumstances, and all will be reflected to you eventually sooner or later.

So here you have it, you need to realize you will have to change your mind! If you have doubts about your life and past performance this is your very first step to do. You, like Madonna need to think that is time to reinvent yourself, that whatever model, ideas, thinking, attitudes of the past you have used have proven their results, and unless you want another 10, 20 or 40 years of the same, you better accept they are outdated.

Let's do the following in order to help you outlining your self-discovery. Do not take more than 5 minutes; just write the first things that come to your mind:

First, make an inventory of your strengths. And for this it can help you to think about those situations where you were in control or achieved results. Think about the times when you have received a commendation, or have been congratulated for a job well done. Play from your memories the times where people seemed to flock to you. What were you doing? How were you communicating with others? What were you wearing? Write them in a piece of paper or better a notebook. Read them aloud. Now, take some time to create an image of you in which you have always been this successful person. You see, everybody has had some measure of success in their lives at one point of time or another. See yourself as you are now and then compare to this new image of you. What do you think prevents you from being like this always? What happened? Write it down.

Next, by now, you must likely know for sure many of your bad character traits. Chances are people close to you have told you many times over your flaws. Are you indecisive? Timid? Afraid to try new things? A capricious spendthrift? Selfish? Procrastinator? Never on time? Or maybe you are on the "over achiever" side with no time for wife/husband or family? If while you go through the list you find and accept you have that obvious certain problem or bad character trait ... no problem! Write down all you remember.

Now, pick your brain to come up with the 10 grandest habits you have. What are the things that you always absolutely completely always do? In reality habits do define a person, and they can be anything such as eating junk food, being a couch potato, always being late, not keeping your promises, etc., etc. write all down.

Now, take a few minutes and cross-reference your lists. Starting from your habits, see if they gravitate or are more alike to your strengths or weaknesses.

Regrettably for most people the habits and the weaknesses have a stronger correlation or similarity than with their strengths. What this means is that you are indeed sabotaging yourself by really acting the opposite of what you are naturally capable to do, and therefore inverting the order of things. I have met people which habits have no correlation with their strengths, or people whom their current job does not even employ any of their strengths.

What you need to do is move step by step to sync your good habits with your strengths.

Keep in mind that the objective of this exercise was to awaken in you the understanding that you need to make some adjustments to your life. You see, as long as you have any strength you really have what it takes to move your life forward, you just need to re-accommodate your items based on new knowledge and create new habits.

Most importantly, no worries, because as you read this book I will give you the tools to start your road to succeed, and you will succeed because you are doing and will do something about it. So keep reading the next steps so you can get the tools you need to start your change,

We will touch more about this in the next chapters, but because I have other things to tell you I will move to other topics, but for now is time to erase what you know and open your mind to accept a new way of thinking and acting.

"People are always blaming their circumstances for what they are. I don't believe in circumstances. The people who get on in this world are the people who get up and look for the circumstances they want, and, if they can't find them, make them."
- George Bernard Shaw

"Never spend your money before you have it"
- Thomas Jefferson

Step 2. Control your money

Money is always an issue. Too little money and problems are sure to rise; you will not be able to make your house or car payment, pay your utilities o even go to the super market to buy essentials, or even worse your wife (or husband) will leave you and take the kids with her/him. However, most people do not know that the opposite is also true. Too much money also brings a myriad of problems to the unaccustomed, you just have to look at the news from time to time and you can see (and probably heard) that many people who come to make a lot of money in very little time such as lottery winners, actors or sports athletes come to lose everything after a few years. Why? that is mainly because people in general do not know how to relate to money, and a sudden and very substantial infusion of money will surely bring imbalance to many people in this world.

As I have observed, regrettably, as humans living in a society, we freely accept the established norms of that society. We do not question mainly what is already there, and worst of all we incorporate that way of doing as correct and we make it part of our thinking.

For example, let's take a look at the accepted notion of the "American Dream". People fail to remember that the American dream is made by you being in debt all your life. When I ask other people about this, they simply do not seem to care. It is fine, "the contract is clear" -They say, "They give me what I want, and I give them my money" or "Hey, I only live once!" I have been told that like an excuse to attempt to have all in life before it ends abruptly. That kind of thinking is now so much part of our culture.

And that seemed to work for me too. I was only forced to change my thinking when disaster stroke. After some very good years, my business failed and I lost everything. I left my home with all I could fit in a rental van which I finished loading at 1:00 am, drove to a storage place and slept there until they opened so I could unload what I was able to salvage.

But no matter, I am a fighter, so I made a plan to very quickly repair my credit and then go to the banks to regain my assets.

I took little things from my storage. So armed with some clothing, my Swiss army knife, my George Foreman grill and my old Nissan, I decided to take life by a storm once again! Forced to take a job, I worked very hard. I shared a room with a good friend of mine for almost a year and later, as I was able to save some money I leased an apartment.

It is in this strange course of events that something extraordinary happened. I saved money! Without me knowing I had changed my habits; for once in my life I only bought what I needed and not what I wanted, why? Because I noticed that what I wanted in many instances was not what I really wanted, but what I had been reinforced over and over I should own. In the past the story went like this... a) boy makes money, b) boy gives money to the banks and c) boy gets in more debt and d) boy keeps $15 dollars (if lucky) at the end of the month. That is not a way to live!

When I looked at my bank account back

then and saw real money I was shocked, but I got the message, I saw the writing in the wall and right then and there my mind changed (and as my mind changed so my actions, and as my actions changed, also my future) and this is what I did next:

First I called my bank and ask for credit and debit card replacements. As the old cards were canceled, suddenly I began to get calls and emails of notices indicating my payment did not go through. This is where it went interesting because I got calls and emails for things I had given my card numbers before for things and services I no longer needed. A magazine subscription, a gym membership that I had not used for years, really expensive accidental insurance... the items just added up and so the savings. At long time past perhaps these things made any sense, but now, nah! I really did not need that.

One summer day I was returning to my job from lunch. While driving suddenly this individual ignores I had the light to turn and hits me full right on the rear door. Needless to say my car was totaled. My insurance gave me about $7,000 dollars. At that time all my friends were driving big brand cars Acura, Mercedes, Lexus... boy I wanted a BMW! And at that time I had enough money to pay at least 20% down payment, so what do you think I did?

Well, I went to Craigslist and look for a used Toyota. I searched and searched until I found a "Dealers Special" it was a 1997 4runner. It was at the corner of the back lot of the dealer. It looked really bad all around, but I had learned my lesson to never judge only by appearance. I asked for the keys, asked for a battery jump, turned it on and let it ran until they moved all the cars that were blocking my way for my drive out. I went under it, over it. Checked for leaks

and signs of overheating, turned the AC...
I knew that 1990's Toyotas had a great
quality and liked it more when I found
that 4runner was also assembled in
Japan. So far so good.

I took it for a test ride. All seemed to be
as I wanted it. I had a good feeling. I
made an offer and walked out paying a
little over $3,400 dollars. I knew what to
do. This truck had been forgotten and
left to the elements it looked worse, a
really great friend of mine gave me a ride
to the dealer to buy it, I remember she
looked at me and asked me – are you
buying that? The truck looked really bad.

I took it to my mechanic. He was
surprised too, but differently, because It
seemed the major mechanical
components had been replaced recently
just as I had noticed, kudos for me! Since
I like taking good care of my things I
proceeded to work my magic, and when
I was done with it no one could believe it

was the same truck. Today I still own it. It has given me so many miles of great service! And most importantly while my friends were stuck with $600 to $800 dollar payments a month for their vehicles, I had zero payment and also ended up saving money from the insurance settlement! Cha-ching!

Among all things I wanted to buy a new place. Things had begun to look great. I thought a home purchase of $250,000 dollars will make me very happy. Time to recover my assets! So I worked the numbers. Down payment 10%=25,000 dollars. Approximate optimistic Monthly payment @ 5% mortgage interest rate (my credit was not good) for 30 years= 1.207.85 dollars per month. Then added my perceived costs of taxes, maintenance, and insurance. Taxes are 3% a year in my jurisdiction. So it will be ($250,000 x 3% = $7,500 dollars a year), for insurance I estimated $100 per month and maintenance and utilties (power, gas and water) about $250/month. My grand total per year was = $26,194.20 and that divided by 12 made my monthly payment = $2,182.85 and that was right where I could afford.

If you have noticed, I calculated an annual house payment amount before I calculated my monthly payment. The reason is because I wanted to compare the following; take a look:

Grand total per year = $26,194.20 x **30** years = **$785, 826!**

Now you see what I mean?

How about this...

30 year total = $785,826 divided by my original price of $250,000 = **3.14**

That means that I could have bought 3.14

houses like the one I bought in the first place!

I know that many people are familiar with this concept, but rarely I see someone acting on it. Buying things with no money makes little sense, but buying things making payments for almost one half of your lifetime is really above and beyond to make banks richer.

Perhaps you wonder now what I did, did I buy the house? because we all need a place to live, right?

Before I bought a property and since I had some money I decided to take a trip to China. As soon as I landed I had culture shock! I expected to land in a third world country and surprise! It looked better than my home city. Very well planned, ample avenues, even buses had TV's. It was just great!

So I immersed in the culture and had

many surprises. One day I went to Wal-Mart. So I expected tons of people, long lines and carts full of things, just like in America. Well... no... it did not work that way. People went in looking to buy what they needed, furthermore, I noticed many people looked at articles closely and took time to decide to buy it or not, perhaps like thinking if they really needed it. People left the store with one shopping bag only (of their own because plastic bags are sold to discourage its consumption and to reduce pollution).

I looked also at real estate in China while I was there. As I made some friends also, I had the opportunity to see how they live. A family of 6 living in a small condo. No problem, you see Chinese people do not have the "safety nets" that we have like Social Security and so on, so they are forced to be savers, space is not much of a problem, the problem is when you have a lot of things – I was told.

That alone, changed my notion of the "awesome Mac-mansion" I should have.

I will tell you more of my experience later, since to this date I have made 5 trips to China.

Once I came back I realized I did not need a big space. So and idea came to me.

I looked for an apartment for sale. I found one that had been in the market for some time that nobody seemed to want. After due diligence, I found the property was owned free and clear by the owner. I prepared an offer with owner financing for a 3 year note with a final balloon payment. He accepted and went to closing at a title company like all normal real estate transactions. My monthly payment came to 572 dollars. All together with taxes insurance and maintenance and utilities my current payment is about 700 dollars.

So if I had bought that house I looked first for 250,000, my payment could have been $2,182.85 vs. 700 dollars a month = total savings of $1,482.85 per month! That amounted to $17,794.20 per year times 30 years equals 533, 826 dollars. If I assume I invest my money on anything that could give me 5% a year I would have amassed in total $1,241,337.45!

I guess by now you can see the picture. As Americans, we have been brainwashed to forget about the realities of future money. Spend now, deal with all later. And this happens because it is embedded in our minds and is part of our culture that everything that happens suddenly is bad. For example a sudden death in a vehicle accident is tragic, but everything that happens slowly over time is OK; so dying in 20 years due to cigarette smoking is fine; we can kill ourselves by over indulging in food or alcohol, no problem! as long as it happens over many years. I could have signed into a $785,000 dollar total debt for the house I wanted, but no worries anyway as long as it happens within 30 years; what? It is nonsense! we are making now financial decisions that are just not sound. Now you can see why my friends never seem to have money; they are giving all to the banks! Whereas me, I live happy and have money, no pressure.

Changes need to happen, and I have given you examples of what I have done that has given me some handsome cash rewards. My life broke down, but I happen to clean the slate and start anew from scratch after no one wanted to lend me anything; as I understood that after all my old thinking was what originally led me to trouble and saw the advantages it has worked out great for me. You can do the same too. Be creative and become a lateral thinker so start thinking about what can you change in your life?

Most people complain about not having enough money, but do not realize the power to take action now, today. They are waiting for a big event (like winning the lottery, befriending a millionaire or inheriting) to change their lives. You need to do something now. Some time ago a friend of mine was telling me that he could not see how he could save for retirement. So I asked him. Do you think you can save 3 dollars? "Probably" -he said. Why do you think is possible for you to save 3 dollars per day? "It is such small amount, surely I can do it" -he replied. So I asked him again, do you think you can save 5 dollars? He nodded. So I told him, if you did that, if you saved 5 dollars a day and you could open an account and get a hypothetical (and exaggerated) 10% return per year, in 20 years you would have 102,701.87 dollars. Now, if your wife could save another 5 dollars you would have $205,403.75! His eyes opened wide...

How did I give that advice? Because I started to do it once I saw the money I had saved. I started to save 5 dollars a day; then I changed my method. As soon as I received a reasonable crispy new bill (those ones that you can still smell the ink) I would put it aside to save it. I got a little box and a paper clip and started. I got 1 dollar here, 5 dollar bill over there, 10 dollar later, 20 dollar bill... I would put them aside in my little box. This did 2 things. I had less to spend because I was taken money out of my pocket and also increased my savings. In a matter of few months I counted the bills... 973 dollars! Wow! I am sure you can find your own method.

Something very important I made a habit of, was that I also decided to carry cash in my pocket. The reason for this is because I noticed that it is really easy to pull a credit or debit card to pay. We are so used to do that the act is inconsequential, but when you spend cash, you can immediately see how your money is running down, and when that happens I knew I had to refrain my expenses.

Now, what you really must know is that most people fail because they believe that nothing can be done and therefore ***they do nothing***! As the ancient proverb says: "the journey of a 1,000 miles start with one step" Your life changes when you move to action and any small change you make over time will make a permanent change in your future if you are constant.

Take a look at your life now. Take a good look at your expenditures. Do you really know where your money went at the end of the month? Do you really need what you want to buy or are you just competing with the Joneses? When was the last time that you prepared a budget? Do you really need all the latest gadgets?

If perhaps you have tried to rein in your finances and you were not able I want you to consider the following too: most of us can actually dismiss anything that is related to will power, because most people do not have it. Not exactly that we are weak, but I have come to realize we tend to succumb to our environment meaning the neighborhood we live in, our co-workers, our family and friends. Real adult peer pressure. Take a look at what surrounds you. Are you constantly being reminded by the people you relate or the environment you are in to spend in one way or another? Just like drinking buddies; if you meet with them, what else are you going to do? Drinking of course! In the same way many times the people you associate with also do influence or determine what you will spend on.

It is on your hands to come out of financial bondage. Do you really need all those credit cards? A few years back I remember a great friend of mine boasting to me he had 75,000 dollars of credit among all the credit cards he had. Of course I knew he had an excellent credit. He was also telling how fast he could summon that money at his command. I remember I asked him, how much cash do you have in the bank? About 4,000 dollars he said. Wow! Worst of all is that he was so proud! I can only imagine making credit card payments on a 75,000 dollar debt...

You do not have to live like a beggar. Just re-visit your objectives and get rid of all the unnecessary baggage you have been carrying for so long.

Also, talking about baggage, chances are that by now you have accumulated a great deal of "things". Get rid of all the clutter that you no longer need. I have gone through my warehouse and have sold most of all I do not need or want.

Some items I have collected for years (my hobby). No matter, I have sold many of them through eBay and surprisingly I have made good money. I have posted also many articles on Craigslist and that has worked really well for me. Now, honestly, I have not regretted any item I chose to sell, at the contrary, I have felt relieved when all those things are gone.

I really want to buy a classic car. But as I see it, with most baby boomers not having enough to retire, increased life spans, decreased home values and a considerable credit card debt accumulated in their peak days, I am perfectly sure that in the few years to come there will be an abundant supply of cheap assets flooding the market. Then I will make my move and will pay cash as well.

Well, it is time for you to take action! Nothing was ever accomplished by doing nothing. Take some time now and sit down and write down your financial objectives. What do you want to achieve? When? Be clear. Then take a look at your recurrent expenditures such as memberships, subscriptions and so on. See what you really need and slash what you don't. Compare electricity providers. Take a new quote for your car and home insurance, take a look at your bank, debit and credit card fees, take notes to see where you money goes. Get rid of all expenses you do not need. If you have not used it, played with it, worn it, activated it, visited, reloaded it in more than a year, trust me, you do not need it. Lastly once you know what you are up against, make a budget and stick to it. Discipline is good, I should have listened to my father who was "old school" and always bought what he needed when he had the money, but I fell into the "American Dream", otherwise, surely, I would be 10 times richer by now.

"We do not stop playing because we grow old; we grow old because we stop playing"
- George Bernard Shaw

"Tell me what you eat, and I will tell you who you are"
- Anthelme Brillat-Savarin

Step 3. Your health. How to feel and look better!

As we were talking about renewal you must know your body needs to be renovated as well. However, here, again, the system that we are playing on is tainted. Out of commerce, American diet is probably one of the worst in the world.

I used to be a thin person. When I came to live permanently in America my eight was about 120 pounds. A few years later my weight sky rocketed to 180 pounds. I was really fat. Not being tall I was miserable.

When my business was coming down, finally I had enough. It was time to change and I decided to take action. Now my weight is 156 pounds and I have kept it for more than 6 years. The good news is that every year I lose more weight gradually.

The first I thing I realized was that I liked chocolate very much. Every day I had to eat 2 full size bars religiously. I was addicted to chocolate. I also liked fast food incredibly much. Of course I knew I was eating too much, but even though I exercised, it was never enough, as a matter of fact every time I exercised I always became hungrier so I actually gained more weight!

So I took action... first I realized that I

had no will power, so what I did was to eliminate my temptations. No more I would buy bags of any type of candy at the supermarket. I also noticed that any kind of change had to have a permanent nature. Anything short term like a diet could only lead me to a partial result, because you only make a temporary change and then go back to your old habits. I resulted to make small changes and I picked 5 things to change.

My number one was to consume no more candy. The number two was to order my hamburgers with no mayo and no cheese. By looking at the McDonald's nutrition tables I calculated that around 1/3 of the calories came from those 2 items. My number 3 was to not to eat until I felt full. I tried to feel when I was satisfied and then do my best to stop eating. Coincidentally, this led to eating less and therefore I had left overs in my plate (against to what I was taught to eat all the food in my plate always). So then, number 3 was changed to always leave left overs in my plate. My number 4 was to avoid big dinners and my number 5 was to try to avoid using my car and start walking.

The result... well think about this... In 6 years of not consuming 2 chocolate bars every day and reducing my fast food intake by 1/3, how many calories have I not eaten? A lot! I just think all those chocolates I did not eat and all those calories I did not intake. As you can see, small changes add up over time. Certainly I did not gain weight overnight, and perhaps neither did you. It was a gradual progression of increased consumption, bad food choices and lower physical activity.

I just want to prove to you that most Americans are stuck in the wrong thinking. Have you ever gone to the supermarket or mall? Of course you have. Have you noticed all this people that circle over and over trying to find the closest spot? I have seen even people fighting because someone else beats them to a parking spot. Now I have the bad habit to look around to see the person if I could and, to my surprise, usually I see an overweighed individual!

For me, I have made it a habit that unless the elements forbid, I shall park away from the rest. For once, I avoid the ding on my car doors, and secondly most importantly, I like now to walk extra. Trust me, and as I have said all adds up to a better me.

Here is something interesting. Going back to China, every time I am there I lose weight. Not only that, I had a gallbladder removal operation about 8 years ago. Since then, I always have some discomfort every time I eat greasy foods. I was surprised when my pain totally disappeared while in China; additionally as you walk around China you very quickly realize that most Chinese are thin. Why? Just look at their diet. Plenty of fish, vegetables, water and tea. It is natural for them to be thin. As I ate what they eat, I used public transportation and walked to my destinations, in a matter of 2 weeks I felt better than ever! Regrettably here in many American cities we have a war with walking and creating great public transportation. Automobiles rule because of the elites that love to import oil and take our money, also keep telling us that driving cars is the only way to go. And we have believed them!

Do you want to make any kind of change permanent in your life? Here is the secret: Start with one small step. Take one item out at a time and stick to avoid its consumption. Do you like soda? Ask for water from now on, or at least from time to time so you do not go "cold turkey". Do you like fast food? Skip the fries, and swap that frozen Frappuccino of about

200 calories for a plain coffee every other day if you are a coffee junkie. Calories not consumed will add up over time. The plain truth is that I saw my life back then I was addicted to the food I ate. I broke the addiction little by little.

Now, let's take action! Make a list of what you must commonly eat. Write in your notebook what you like the most and how often you eat it. Write also how you feel after you eat those items (this will be an eye opener for you). Then select one item and make it a habit to avoid it. Then as you progress you can add another one. As time goes by, you will realize you do not need that item anymore and you have lost the craving for it as well.

Changing your Image

"Fashion fades, only style remains the same"
- Coco Channel

The Captain of your life

Once I lost weight I decided to change the way I look. I thought I was a well-dressed person when I was forced to take job. I was proud of myself until a younger co-worker criticized me. It really took me a while to digest his comments, especially when he told me that he could deduct my age by the clothes I wore. What? Me? Impossible! I thought then I dressed conservatively, timeless. He is wrong!

As time passed by and as most people in my department were younger than me, finally I opened to question my accepted conventions, gave him the benefit of the doubt and decided to observe what he wore every day. Then I looked into magazines to see what was advertised for men my age. After a month I realized what he meant. So I called him one day and humbly asked him: How much do you think I need to change the way I look? He answered really fast, and started spilling the beans while I took careful notes. "You can start with less than 400 dollars" -he said. I was really surprised to hear that you can do it a complete change of wardrobe for so little.

Next I incorporated his concepts into what I had researched. I really was looking to improve all that I could improve about myself. I needed a holistic approach, because what good will it do to dress very well if I have bad breath! So here are the pointers I got for me from his instructions and my observations.

For men:

1. Unless you are really overweight, never wear your pants at your belly button level. It destroys the natural shape of the men's body if you are reasonably shaped. Wear them at the waist.

2. Find shirts that fit. Never buy a shirt

that is really tight (unless you are full of muscles) or worst, never buy a shirt that is cut the "American" way; that is like a sack of potatoes with sleeves. Even if you are overweight, you need to show your basic shape.

3. Get a good pair of shoes. For starters your feet will thank you. Your shoes say a lot about you if they come to be in the field of view of the person you are with. Worn out, dirty, damaged or discolored shoes make you look cheap or at least messy, just like having long nails. Trust me; women take a look at your feet and hands. Also, in regards to your shoes, very importantly, give them a good shoe shine from time to time. Nothing beats a properly dressed man with shiny shoes. Wearing a great outfit with old or dirty shoes will suggest that maybe you borrowed the clothes from your brother who does happen to have style.

4. Shave. Unless your wife or girlfriend

has told you she likes the sand paper feeling of your face, thou shall always shave.

5. Make your teeth look good. Yellow, brown or otherwise discolored or chipped teeth make you look older and unhealthy. Brighten your smile and open your mouth with confidence. Personally I like my sonic tooth brush and my water pick. Both do clean better and deeper and make my teeth look whiter. Floss often and visit your dentist for regular teeth cleaning.

6. Get a haircut regularly. Unless you look like Brad Pitt or Einstein, I really suggest you to have a haircut at least once every two weeks.

7. If you happen to want to buy a new wardrobe, follow this simple advice:

Once you have gone to the mall or check different stores and have found what clothes fit you (this may take some experimenting). Then just buy the normal palette of colors for shirts and pants. If you are just beginning, just buy plain colors. Black, charcoal, navy blue (light blue shirt), gray, brown. Do not buy patterns yet because they are more noticeable and you will need more money. Most importantly is that you can combine them. Black pants with light blue shirt. Black shirt with gray pants, Charcoal pants with navy blue shirt... you get the point. You can buy also a trendy belt. Most people keep their belts forever and I do not know why. If your belt has rendered you with years and years of faithful service and is worn out and has lost its color, or you have fixed it more than 2 times, trust me, it is time to retire it then. Prepare a ceremony and decommission it.

8. Lastly, Exercise. Same thing here, not that you have to prepare for a marathon. Just change your mentality to start moving. In the company I used to work for we had free coffee. I would take the long route to get to the kitchen. Instead of bringing my large jug of water, I swapped it for a glass, and what this achieved is that I would have to go more times to the kitchen for a refill. I would park my car farther to walk a little more. If I had documents to deliver I would not use the intra-mail, I would walk to the office of the person and drop them myself depending on time. Little changes every day worked great for me, and I always enjoyed the little break.

For Women:

Women are at a different league because there is so much they can do than men cannot in regards to their looks and this is great.

A woman can, effectively conceal her defects and enhance her virtues. Fashion and culture have given that prerogative to women; it is a big, big plus. A woman can make her eyes look bigger her cheekbones look fuller just by using makeup, or even increase her height using high heels as examples.

So here are some tips to improve yourself.

1. Find what fits you.

What really takes women apart from men is the woman's curvy body. Using clothes that are too small that you can barely breathe really looks bad in front of most men. It just looks like when you heat milk and it spills out. Also, using clothes that are too big will make you look like a 2 liter soda pop bottle. What you need is clothing that clings to your body and shows your curves. If you put it on and you feel good and beautiful, most probably it is so. Even if you are extremely thin or overweight, buy clothes that give definition to your waist to define your shape.

2. Be natural with makeup.

Excess of color will undo you. I sincerely recommend most women to visit a professional that will tell them what goes good with their skin tone and their face shape. Ask questions when he/she is working on you. Ask for different looks like Casual, office and night out makeup. Also ask how to apply simple makeup when you are in a hurry; what simple touches you need to do in order to look presentable without taking a lot of time.

If you are not happy with the advice then try someone else, but at the end I know you will get great knowledge and you will look great!

3. Fashion comes and goes. Be bold and create your own sense of style but dress your age. You see, by combining elements that go well with your type of body along with using accessories that accent your personality, you create your own image. You do not have to spend a fortune either. Just a few days ago I saw a woman that looked awesome with the right pair of jeans, a nice blouse and heels. She had a scarf on that gave her distinction. She knew how to wear a scarf. She did a great job to know what fits her and men were looking (me included).

4. Look good for your husband. This might will sound stupid, but trust me, it is very important. We, that is men, are 1000% visual creatures, and mostly

wherever we go there is women around and we like to look. In all my life I have seen that as people are more entrenched in a relationship, or have been in a marriage for a long long time they just take each other for granted. There is no real reason to excel for someone who you see every day right? Wrong!

I know that when children appear things get hectic, but me as a man I can tell you from my experience, when even though marriage and kids I have seen couples that still take time to look good for one another it makes me smile.

In my personal opinion dressing well it is a sign of respect to your spouse that says I care to look good for you because I want you to want me.

5. Stay away from the drama. Take a look at this:

"It is better to dwell in the corner of the housetop, than with a brawling woman in a wide house
- Proverbs 25:24 KJV

Nothing keeps away a man from a woman than the constant nagging of a wife or partner. For some reason some women have misunderstood that yelling and constantly screaming or mistreating a man does bring a position of equality from which an advantage can be obtained. Nothing can be farther than the truth; if you want respect, you need to give respect. I have friends that rather not go home than face the wrath and nagging of their wives. They know they have messed up, but yet they know what is waiting for them and they will do all they can to avoid it until things get cooler.

If you really want to produce a change in your man, never engage when you are angry, a verbal frontal attack is not advisable, even if you win, you will destroy your man's ego. The arsenal and weaponry of a woman is not on her muscles, but in her charms, intuition and intellect. If you think you are right then have a serious conversation and get to an agreement. Do tell your husband what will happen if his conduct or actions return, but then stick to what you have said you will do, and do it. A loving partner will work for you and even ask for your help to advance because he knows he made a mistake and would not like to lose you. If you can succeed together it will even be a greater victory and will strengthen your relationship, however, if it does not go that way then you have your answer about what to do.

Also, please, do not forget to listen to him as well. You might be overstretching or overreaching or maybe wrong in your appreciation and maybe you need to change as well. Be willing and open to compromise

6. Get closer to him and what he likes. Nothing makes a guy look cooler, than when his woman has an interest on what he does and other men observe. I have played video games, fantasy cards and even do car mechanics along with the women of close friends and it has been a lot of fun together.

See what you can do, you do not have to fake it, just have a genuine interest on what he likes and who knows... maybe when you understand why he likes what he likes, you may even like it as well.

You will do well to include him in what you like too. I used to hate antiques searching and looking until my girlfriend explained with so much veracity an old meat grinder. I liked that and we passed great times traveling around just looking at stuff.

7. Move away from any type of abuse. If you are abused in any way or manner and you have tried to make these offenses stop but you have not been successful, you need to walk away!

You need to understand that there are certain men that will never change. Do not attempt to save the world and sacrifice yourself to gain his soul. It does not work like this. Seek immediate help.

"The secret of many a man's success in the world resides in his insight into the moods of men and his tact in dealing with them"
- J. G. Holland

"Arguing with a fool proves there are two"
- Doris M. Smith

Step 4. Improve your relationships.

Nothing in this life impacts your life more than your relationships. If you know the right people the world credentials of grand education or even proficiency will matter less or none at all. It is true; in many instances it is not who you are, but who you know what will make you successful.

As a matter of fact I can tell you that if you want to measure how much your life will improve in the next 5 years I will tell you that it will be in direct relation with a) the new knowledge you acquire during that time, b) the cultivation and improvement of the relations with the people you know now along with creation of new friendships, and c) how much you change your mind, take action and create new habits based on that knowledge and influence.

What pulls you forward are your resources, but resources not used are just potential energy. Your resources need to convert into something tangible that leads you to a defined action, and in this case, knowledge, people and you, pulling in the same direction. If you can do that, then you can bet your engine is firing on all pistons... shoot to the moon then!

But perhaps at this moment you may think I will write about third party individuals you should influence like your co-workers or friends. Nope, at least not yet. I need to write first about the people that are closest to you. Yes, I am talking about your wife or husband. The most important relationship you have is probably the one that is most overlooked.

Your wife (or husband) is the person who is closest to you. You have chosen each other to share a life together. He or she is your grandest ally, but can also drag you down to the bottom of the ocean if you have a bad relationship.

I have talked to all of my friends about this. I have seen many relationships in the making. As humans we seem to have figure out the mechanics of courtship, but once real life sets in we all seem to go our own way.

At the time of this writing the US is probably one of the top 5 countries with the highest divorce rates in the world. Why, I wondered? What are the parts in our culture that makes walk out of a marriage with the person we some time before we said that could not live without? All things being equal some very interested facts I came to discover.

The number one thing I have discovered is that we have become more and more a selfish society. On top of that we are reminded every day by the powers on top of how we all are different and hence we should not unite but it is better to be divided. Your things are yours; my things are mine. Then, when we add the taboos of religion, the hectic jobs we have, our financial habits and the duties and obligations we have to carry for our children, extended families and social life, this leaves small time left to improve a relationship. We are just too busy.

Contrary to what we did when we started courting our partner, when we wanted to spend all the time with them and spent countless hours talking about plans and the future, now that usually disappears as the years go by. As I told you before to look good for your partner, now I can add to take time to be with your partner. Communication is always key, but communication is not a matter of saying what you think on top of your mind. We, as people require diplomacy and more than anything respect to deal with one another, and regrettably respect is the one thing that has gone away as our civilization and culture plows into the future. This is indeed very important. We demonstrate our disrespect when we say to our partner we will arrive at a certain hour, but we arrive late citing "a lot of work", when we "forget" important things and dates, when we fail to listen to the claims or suggestions we are told because its "football" time... Well you get the point.

This is very important because well inside ourselves we know how to automatically irk those who we love. Since we have been with them in intimacy and together too long we know where their soft nerves are, but yet some times we do very little to concede when we are wrong or just do something to please them. "Let them please me first and then I will do it..." –we say.

If you have problems in this area you need to reinstate respect. You can define it like this: You will do what you said you will do and you will communicate in a civilized manner. The funny thing about it is that as long as your wife or husband keep getting mad with you because you fail to fulfill your duties or promises, that still is an indication that there is still affection from them to you. I have seen the other side of the coin, when no matter what you do, your wife or husband will not say a word of reproach to you, and the reason is that they got so tired of you that at that point they really do not care for you anymore; you might as well die and they will not care, just like in Gone with the Wind when Clark Gable said to Vivien Leigh when she asks him what will she do after he leaves her and he responds: "Frankly my dear, I do not give a damn".

Respect opens the communication lines. Usually is the men the one that proposes matrimony, but men must remember that a woman accepted this proposal based on what he did before marriage.

As for you, even as time changes and many things evolve, there are many things you did then that your wife or husband still likes, it is best when two people evolve together at the same time, and it will do you much good if you find those things and revisit it them with your wife/husband. Perhaps you can find together the way to bring in a new way that still says that you care and do not take for granted your relationship.

The bible says in Amos 3:3 "can two walk together unless they agree?" Certainly not, but as long as they are walking together they can still talk to each other and get to agree, so there is hope.

Pay attention to your partner. Do take time to listen to his/her complaints. Walk the extra mile if you can to help or please her. Open the communication lines and take time for each other.

Some words about sex...

> "I know nothing about sex, because
> I was always married"
> - Zsa Zsa Gabor

In other area, sex is very important in any relationship. Regrettably because of our religious beliefs and inherited culture we really must find about it by practice. Women do not know, but I think most contemporary men were educated watching porno, or listening to other friends that "had some experience". In reality I did not get to know how really women work and feel until a lot of time passed and was young no longer. The reason why I decided to learn was of my own to have a real fulfilled sex life.

I have an open mind, and I love learning new things. One of my hobbies is to ask questions about taboos when the situation allows. I get along great with mostly everybody, but for some reason I feel better being among women, so I have queried the entire establishment I have had access to.

So when men talk about what they like about women, I have realized that we all are so very different. Some men like boobs, some like feet, some like legs... we all are turned on by different things, but when I ask the question to men if their wives know what they like; depending of how weird it is the thing they like usually the answer is no. For women it is even deeper, in my experience I have found that women are more sexual creatures than men ultimately; many women are just like a Pandora's Box that once opened it cannot be stopped; but as our culture has evolved I find women are more restricted to explore their sexuality or to try and expose what is on their minds to their partners.

In this world rarely things are instant. For most things we need to wait a long time to get a result. We work for 2 weeks to get paid, we wait 6 months (maybe longer) to get a vacation, we wait 15 to 30 years to own a home... well, very few things bring you an instant sure reward. Sex is one of the very few things in life that will give instant pleasure for sure if done correctly. The problem is that we all are wired and programmed differently, so it is in our best interest to get to know our partner and find how get our wires together.

Sex is created for intimate pleasure. It also brings you closer to your partner and enhances your relationship if it brings pleasure to both partners. The bible is for it:

> "Do not deprive of each other perhaps by mutual consent and for a time, so that you may devote to prayer. Then come together again..."
> (1 Corinthians 7:5 NIV)

I am lucky that after my research my sexual life has been very satisfying and here is my advice:

Men and women have different sexual timing, men gets to climax faster. In order for me to avoid getting to the finish line first, what I do is to work to please her before me. So in the order of things she comes first (literally) and then you. If you change your thinking about this, this means you will have to find out what your partner likes and also get to know when she finishes. Even if you as a man have had experience with a lot of women, I can tell you that all women are different, it is worse if you assume you know your wife or partner, it is wise to explore. In fact I have not found 2 women that like exactly the same, so is your duty to know how her machine works!

I have literally spent a lot of time to be able to break the barrier to ask and understand what my darling wants. So I sit down and ask, "...tell me what you like, truly, the more honest you are the more you will enjoy it". I have taken the best opportunities to do that. Taking a trip out of the city, inviting her to a nice dinner, having some drinks, or just walks hand in hand. I am a caring person and do listen. The results are awesome, if you have truly pleased your wife; she will do wonders to please you!

Not only men and women have different climax timing, but also we men like to have sex as frequent as possible. Women have different cycles when they want sex. I know that if men could take more time to understand and really work to please women first, it would be otherwise easier for men to get more frequent sex, especially when a woman takes the time to please her man besides having intercourse.

Once I had a relationship with a very successful business woman. She mentioned to me that she was afraid of sex and usually she needed lubricant in advance of sex. I asked her what she liked and took my time to please her. It really worked out really good. She mentioned afterwards that she always thought of sex as a chore and never really got to enjoy it, but she was glad that she then could feel normal and use no lubricant. Of course this takes time to discover and agree what makes one another tick, but it is so important that many a marriage have been destroyed because of failure in this aspect of life, especially when the answer is simple, but it gets hard because of our wrong beliefs. Remember that a partner that has not sexual fulfillment may look for that fulfillment elsewhere, so it is worth it to make an effort.

It is time to get away from taboos and find and discover how to mutually achieve a higher level of sexual pleasure; if after all we fail to communicate because of our old ideas and concepts we inherited from people and circumstances past, then, as I have mentioned, you can expect your next 20 years to be as sexually as "rewarding" as what you have experienced. Get it? Easy does it, if you have a genuine interest you will find a way, but nothing will happen until you take the first step.

One big word of advice. Never, ever get discouraged. Very rarely anything was achieved when done the first time. Persevere, be creative, and never surrender. The rewards are astonishing. Why do people leave each other? Because they stopped caring, listening, sharing with one another; they stopped having things in common. If you really care for your relationship to last, you must remember how it was at the beginning; more so, how you were at the beginning, what changed? Find out, make changes, live a better life (and get lucky at the same time!)

> "Sex is not the answer. Sex is the question. "Yes" is the answer"
> - Swami X

"We pretend to work because they pretend to pay us"
-Unknown

"A well paid 5 hour workday will make any country the most efficient and best in the world"
- Gustavo Alberto Hernandez

Step 5. Take control of your work life.

Things have changed very much in America in the last 10 years. The many bust cycles that brought the destruction of equity in the markets and people's retirement and savings have produced permanent changes in the work environment. Companies are not hiring as they used to and they are demanding more work from their employees for the sake of "efficiency". Long are the boom days where promotions benefits increased as companies expanded.

I have worked for fortune 500 companies mostly in my life. In the boom years I was very satisfied because I moved up in my career by responding to challenges and being rewarded by solving them. But besides for the times when moving through the corporate ladder was fun for me and was given the resources I wanted in return for positive results, now things have changed for the worse.

But to tell you the truth I never liked the American way of working. Since I can remember I have always been able to do my job in 6 hours or less a day except when I move to other industries and need to catch up fast learning my new job. Provided I get what I ask, I can learn and catch up really fast. The normal 8 to

5 does not really work for me and never has.

In my last job, I had to learn a new industry. But soon I caught in what I wanted to do, kept my desk clean and my tasks done. My reward? I was given more work. Boomer!

On the other hand, having a job can be also rewarding, if depending on your abilities, character and environment, you have: a) a channel to contribute to the organization, b) a chance to improve your skills, c) you have a real manager (or Director, or VP) that understands what is important and knows how to treat an organization and people, d) a good remuneration and benefits.

But here I am going to write about what to do to improve your career and put it on track to succeed, and also, will tell you how to recognize if you are stuck in the wrong place and the strategies you can utilize to find your right path.

So let's begin:

>1. *Define what you want in your career.* This may seem pretty obvious but most people do not have a clear path of what they clearly want and much less when they want it. Most people profess that they want better pay, promotions or so on, but very few people indeed have a clear pathway on how and when they want to achieve it. Take time and think, see how you would like to see yourself in the next 3, 5 or 10 years. What position you want and why you want it. This also includes maybe moving to another division or changing to that other company you

always wanted to work for and even starting a new career. Write it all down.

2. Find your work strengths. Take some time and analyze what are the things that you do better than anyone else. Are you a fast thinker? Can you come up with creative solutions no matter what the problem is? Do you speak other languages? Are you good talking and relating to people? There is no right or wrong answer, write all down in your notebook.

3. Match your strengths to your job. Do any of your current job activities mirror your strengths or give you an opportunity to exercise your strengths? Make a model, a matrix, and brainstorm and see the inter-relationships between one another. Also see if your strengths match another position or job you might be interested.

4. Find your weaknesses. Same thing here. Write down all the things that you are no good or very little good at such as being disorganized; being never on time and so on... Write it down.

5. Match you weaknesses to your job. Make your matrix model and cross reference with your bad traits.

Now you have pretty good map of your abilities vs. your working reality. If you have more cross references from your weaknesses to your job tasks, you must have it pretty miserable. It also works the other way around, if you have more strengths than what you are doing you maybe wasting yourself. But the point here is dual. If you are really weak in a certain area, and that is required in your job in order to be successful, then you know you need to make your weakness a strength. For example if you job requires to give presentations from time to time but you are afraid of public speaking, then you know you have to improve in this area, or you can be creative and talk to your boss or co-worker to swap this duty for another in which you are good. The other objective is to see if one of your strengths can overcome one of your weaknesses. For example if you have no good analytical skills, but you are an organized person, perhaps you can create a checklist to have your job done and create an electronic spreadsheet with additional checks and balances to verify your work. Be creative, always be creative; you can improve your work life just by simply adapting, assimilating and then transforming yourself based on that knowledge.

What you have written before in your notebook has been an effort to help you get to discover more about yourself and the intrinsic relation with the activities you perform in your job and how, with some creativity you should re-accommodate your activities to your benefit; if you cannot go through straight, then go around.

Additionally, there are other elements besides you knowing yourself that you should know. I am convinced that the variables that will make you successful in any job are the following, take a look:

1. Practice good office politics. It really does not matter how good you are and how good you can do your job if you are disliked or are always away from the action in the fringe lines of your department. Make yourself available and be congenial as much as you can with everyone, but at the same time be cunning by not revealing your cards and like chess thinking several steps ahead what is to happen in your organization and what you will do to benefit. Practice diplomacy, which most people do not know anything about. Diplomacy is "...the employment of tact to gain a strategic advantage or to find mutually acceptable solutions to a common challenge, one set of tools being the phrasing of statements in a non-confrontational, or polite manner." (Wikipedia, Diplomacy. 5-25-12).

Most people fail here because they go to work day by day with the wrong attitude and thinking they are always right and the others aren't, the goal here is to achieve that, when people mention your name, something positive is said, that you make a great impression with anyone. Trust me, it will come handy.

2. Only fight the wars you can win. Conflict is unavoidable, it will happen with other members and even superiors in your organization. Regrettably, people's egos are very frail, so you must be careful, but most importantly, you need to protect your reputation as someone who gets things done and do not waste time. Hence in any conflict or dispute only fight (and be diplomatic about it, of course!) the ones you are for sure to win. It is worthless to fight with someone or about something if you will lose even if you are right; better to move away and live to fight another day.

3. Promptly accept your mistakes and come with a suggestion or action plan to correct the deficiency. Nothing is worse in my experience than hearing people attempting to shift the blame, or denying what is obvious. Additionally, if you know that an error has been made by you or the people at your command below you, promptly tell the powers above you about it. Trust me, what people in the upper levels hate the most is the surprise, and that is when someone else from another department or his/her boss finds an error that you or your organization made and your boss knew nothing about it. Better is when other party communicates the error and your boss' reply is that he is aware of it and it is being worked, as he speaks to be corrected.

4. Stay away from negative and whining people. Do not associate with them. If you listen to them, little by little, day by day they will drag you to the bottom along with them. These people usually amount to nothing so keep your distance. Associate with the positive people; yes the ones that see an opportunity in any challenge, learn from them, assimilate and transform your thinking.

5. Refrain from openly criticizing anyone. Listen to me on this one. If you say something bad about a co-worker or your boss, sooner or later it will echo around revised and expanded. Do not trust to have any confidentiality about your expressed opinions. Very rarely any individual or manager or director will react positively to any critique given by you or anyone especially if it is a lower ranked person. When commenting on something negative, be ambiguous... "yes I believe the results were discouraging, surely the method can be improved... I will pass my ideas later". Listen to others for information but remain neutral as Switzerland in WWII, let the other powers fight and kill each other and then negotiate with the winner. Take a look at the following piece of advice:

"Criticism of others is futile and if you indulge in it often you should be warned that it can be fatal to your career"
- Dale Carnegie

6. Invest in yourself. More and more in the US I realize we are looking more like a third world country. You see, because there are fewer jobs in relation to the work force pool in those countries, people in there really strive to get more education in order to land a job. You will find a lot of individuals with MBA's and PHD's because they need to get ahead of the rest. Furthermore, job openings do require these high levels of education because they can get to the top of the pool and pick the best of the best. Take a look at India as an example.

In the US I find now that as the pool of work is reduced year after year, Not only MBA's are required, but also any 3 world letter as well. CIA's, CMA's, CFA's... you name it.

If you are fixed to continue advancing in your career, it is necessary you take any and all advantages to increase your knowledge and separate yourself from the rest. This is not a request, but is mandatory specially because the pool of work will continue to reduce as American consumption decreases and personal debt spirals out of control, or at least takes a big bite when individuals deal with repaying that debt. Believe me; the next 10 years will be tough. So take advantage of any opportunity; this includes paid education plans from your company, or working separate on your own to obtain special qualifications and degrees. The thing here is that whatever you achieve is totally yours to keep. It increases your value and when added to your experience and success, makes you more desirable. Successful, well poised and credentialed individuals are always sought no matter what the times are. Otherwise there would be no more head hunters.

7. Make yourself available. People on top like to count on other people to get their job done. Volunteer to special projects or individually or electronically comment with your boss about ideas you have for improvement. Be vocal about this not making emphasis on how good you are, but on how it will benefit your manger's department or division.

Now, here is the last part of this section. I am going to write to you about something that you need to keep in mind and that most people overlook. You need to come to understand your vocation and abilities. Most people's errors are here. We are all different, but thankfully we all have different abilities. One of the major problems is when a person takes a job because of "that is where the money is" or based on what your parents decided it was best for you.

Every day I face an incredible amount of individuals that clearly do not have the vocation to do their jobs. For example, the medical industry. Careless, dispassionate and bad service is the norm. Have you waited in an emergency room lately? It is clear that besides the people who really have a real vocation to serve there, many individuals are there because of job security. And you can see it in their frustrated faces, lack of attention, bad humor and bad service.

Same happens in the airline industry. I fly quite often and away from the times I fly in business class, my personal experience is about 8 out of 10 times the service is bad or non-impressive. Airlines from the US used to be number one in service, now as they have been in so much trouble I believe the number one cause is because the service is bad. The best airline I have ever flown is Emirates.

Asian airlines are really good too. I happened to be in a flight to Dubai and no matter what I asked; I was constantly answered with a smile. Out of time from the meal service, I asked for a juice. The flight attendant came back with a big smile and two glasses of juice instead of one, she made eye contact with me, asked me if I wanted to recline my seat further to be more comfortable. That is service!

From here, I can see that is very clear that most people do not go according to their vocations but follow the crowd into something they could do or had to take a pick on a career that closely resembled what they liked. Then they go to corporate America and they see their careers stagnating and then wonder why their careers do not advance.

It is here when I need to be frank with you. There is a big difference with having a job, being on line to make a career and following your passion.

Having a job is just having the means to obtain an income. You just do it for the money and nothing else. If anyone offers you more money you will certainly leave on the spot, bye bye miserable job!

Having or making a career is more than having a job. This means you are seriously committing your time, energy and resources to advance within a certain organization in return for some financial reward/recognition/promotion/ or retirement package.

Following your passion is another story. Usually your passion will be what you like doing always and what gives you meaning to your life. You could do it with or without remuneration (and ironically it is usually what you plan to do when you retire).

I have written you the steps to succeed

in your job along with the strategies you could follow up to ramp up your exposure and increase your performance; however do take in consideration that it may happen to you like happened to me. I used to have a job. A job in which I wanted to make a career. But my passion is to be creative, to make my job easier, to increase my knowledge, to relate to people, to synchronize resources and systems to get rid of major B.S. and get things better.

You may think that what I am writing you about what I wanted to do were great tools for any organization to have, but much to my surprise I was cut off at every corner. I knew what was my priority and the variables that were to advance my career and the group, however, the division I worked for were stuck in another paradigm; suggestions meant nothing unless they came from above, they were more interested in shuffling tasks than improving them.

This in turn put a lid on my creativity and effectively rendered me useless. Soon after I started to get sick, and sicker until I could handle it no more.

Today as I look back I realize I needed to get out of that. The group I worked for was not a match for me. I have always had passion on what I do. The lesson I learned is that I would follow my passion until that would be all I could do. You as well need to sit down and assess your life, step out of yourself and from a distance see if you are working on what really gives meaning to your life.

Once I recognized my new reality that is the time when my revival began! And now I follow my passions such as writing, which is something I always wanted to do, and you see while you work on what you really like, suddenly your life changes, it becomes better and fuller. Now, no matter what happens I am happy working on the things I like. Since my expenses are low and I have saved money based on the advice I have given you, I can follow my passion; can you follow yours? Well, if you follow the steps I lined up for you previously you could very well on your way to do what I am doing in little time!

"Never continue in a job you don't enjoy. If you are happy in what you are doing, you'll like yourself, you'll have inner peace. And if you have that, along with physical health, you will have more success than you can possibly have imagined"
- Johnny Carson

"Consult not your fears but your but your hopes and your dreams. Think not about your frustrations, but about your unfulfilled potential. Concern yourself not with what you tried and failed in, but with what is possible for you to do"
- Pope John XXIII

"If you surrender to the wind, you can ride it"
- Tony Morrison

"Happiness is a choice. You grieve, you stomp your feet, you pick   yourself up and choose to be happy"
- Lucy Lawless

Step 6. Close the door to your past (and weld the door shut)

You have made great progress until here. You have taken a look to your financial situation, your health, your relationships and your job. You have decided to make changes, small changes at the beginning but lasting and constant changes that will bring deep and permanent positive changes in your life.

I knew I could not address total success in my life if I could not release my "baggage". So, if you like most people are still are carrying the heavy burden of your life past, or that one thing you have not exactly forgiven yourself for, or another person who did something to you, then we need to address that now.

Divorce, failure, self-punishment, anguish, anxiety for all the sins we have committed in our life, we are so no deserving...

But I tell you, even if you have failed in all areas... no sweat! You have to think that if you are reading this book that means that all and everything you have done in your life has brought you to this moment; if we sum all your life the results will end up here; you with me sharing this moment while you read this book.

I do not really care what brought you here, the only thing I care is that you are here; you made it! You see, I care less how you got to this point, because what I do care is about the power you have to do the things you want and need to do from this point forward. That is all that is important, the past is gone and it is only a part of your memory, but your future, that, we can build.

Just imagine this. Imagine that you are driving your car on a rainy Friday night; suddenly you lose control and crash. You have hit your head and you lost your memory. Now, someone enters and tells you that you are a famous and successful entrepreneur. He goes on to show you your accomplishments, the content of your character and the ideas you live and die for. Since you have no memory (no field of reference), based on what you have been told, do you think once you come out of the hospital, would you be a different person? Do you think you would act differently? Do you think you will make different decisions and therefore change your future? I bet you will!

You see, regrettably it is ingrained in our beliefs that we always must bear eternal punishment for all bad we have done and deserve eternal remorse for our past actions and mistakes, we must repent and pay the price, because who knows when, and if we will ever be forgiven, right?

But I tell you my dear friend that you like everyone else, you probably have paid the price already for what you did because it is almost impossible to not to generate a reaction that will affect us when we wrong somebody. So if you are thinking about your broken marriage, the friend you cheated, the money you wasted, you have paid some price already by losing your life partner, in the cheating, well, you lost your friend, and your punishment for wasting money is that you have it no longer.

For those who genuinely know they messed up, there is a solution:

We all have our regrets including me, and one day while exploring the mechanics of finding relief to my life; I was reading the bible and bumped into something interesting. It was about the word "repent" in the following verse where Jesus is speaking to his disciples:

> "Jesus answered; Do you think that these Galileans were worse sinners than all the other Galileans because they suffered this way? I tell you, no! But unless you repent, you too will all perish" (Luke 13:2 and 3 NIV)

You see, so as I read, it is clear that everyone must repent. Actually, you better repent, or else... but how to repent and get relief? That was my question...

Perhaps I got the answer as a revelation, but all came clear to me when I realized what is that God really wanted; you see, the key is in what Jesus said; or better said, on what it is that he really said. As it is written in the New Testament the word "Repent" actually comes from the Greek word "metanoia"   which means **_"change of mind"._**

When I read that, then BUM!!! I got it! I cannot tell you how good I felt when I realized I had been wrong all my life, because in reality If God wants anything from you after you have failed miserably and you have acknowledged it, is that you learn from your experience and you change your mind! Changing your mind meaning   throwing   away   your   old thinking, which in reality is what got you in trouble in the first time!

Repenting is really not about the tears, the anguish we feel or having remorse all our life, repenting is about understanding we did wrong and then change our mind to not to ever do it again. Only in this way, by learning from your mistakes you can truly keep on living, because whether you like it or not we will always make mistakes, but what makes us better people is when we learn from our mistakes and evolve from them, because it was never meant for us to dwell in our failure forever, otherwise personal growth would be impossible!

So there you are... it is time for you to move on. Have you learned your lesson? Then is time for you to change your mind and better yourself.

Now, something very important I need to tell you as well. We must balance the equation; you must never forget that to be forgiven, one must forgive. Only when you forgive others you can be forgiven. In Korea they have a say: "to cover with mud your neighbor's face, you must first mud your hands" So I tell you: let all evil go, or else it will touch you first. If you can practice restitution (very important), then do so. If not, but you have tried, then then let it be so.

The options is yours and always in your hand, and this is because life is nothing but a collection of experiences that you acquire since you are a baby to the end of your life, and those experiences will keep happening as long as you breathe; what you do with those experiences whether if they are positive or negative is and will always be up to you.

So today I tell you: Change your mind, forgive, act differently and move forward to create your new future!

"There are many who are living far below their possibilities because they are continually handling over their individualities to others. Do you want to be a power in the world? Then be yourself. Be true to the highest within your soul and then allow yourself to be governed by no customs or conventionalities or arbitrary man-made rules that are not founded in principle"
- Ralph Waldo Trine

Step 7. Wake up your hidden potential.

So far, so good. Before you were reading this book you were set in your ways, and you could not define the direction you wanted your life to take. Now, you have new ideas and have set tasks that little by little will yield the results to improve and get a more fulfilling life.

However, what I have given you are only the mechanics to deal with your stagnant life and move you forward in the environment you currently live to develop within. But the real gem lies further than that.

I am convinced that one of the greatest illusions that we live in our times, is that we have bought in the great American society dream, but do not get me wrong, for me, America is the greatest country in the world, even though I can clearly see we are on the wrong path because our true values have been hijacked by people that have nothing to do with the values you and I live for. They have imposed their values which have all to do with power, greed, misinformation, denial... in short they practice and do only what serves their own purpose.

Therefore, the first thing I want to tell you is that it is necessary that you question everything. Do not believe that anyone will take care of you, and much less our government which is in a serious need to be overhauled. Regrettably the four columns that supported this great nation in regards to our financial future have been deliberately detonated. You see In the past you could reasonably assume you could be ahead of the game after working your tail off because you had your Social Security pension, then you had your 401K, then your company's pension plan and last but not least the equity in your home. Now, think social security? Maybe 30 cents per every dollar I put in I will get back, who knows? Your 401k for sure has taken a beating in the last 10 years, and guess what? we are heading for more declines ahead; company pension plan? Most retirement plans are underfunded and many companies now do not offer pensions anymore; lastly your home equity... I tell you, do not count on it to appreciate like it happened in the past, or think you may cash out/sell or refinance any time you want. Hence you must be an active participant in our society, especially as we demand the return of good values to public and private life.

Same happens with your job. In my travels I see that many people still live now with a 50's mentality in which they still believe in American companies and the promises they make. They believe that the contract that once existed of loyalty between an employee and employer goes on even in a reduced version; that they will take care of us and that we could work all our lives and have a lifetime of achievements and recognition. I once worked for a construction firm in which 3 generations of the same family had worked for the same company, wow! But then came the Wall Street people, and changed laws and regulations and companies started to manage their stock instead of managing their companies! I saw that happening... "let's be all as creative we can be, but not to create a better product or service or take care of our employees, but to see how we can extract that extra penny per share to meet or beat expectations" That was the beginning of our financial moral decline in my opinion. Therefore, do not let anybody choose for you; demand what is best for you in your work, your family, our city and our country.

The second thing I want you to know and away from the social part is this:

Remember when you were young or a kid? Remember how you used to think? Remember the things you liked? Can you compare yourself now with whom you were then? Do you remember the dreams you had then? Whatever you have become, probably you had deviated from the original idea you had. Revisit your life and memories and see if you can revive your original goals and dreams. Do not waste your time watching TV once you come from work, or if you must watch, then limit your time, then go to your room or studio or wherever you feel good and see if you can put some effort day by day to write and define how to make your dream a reality.

Once you have tuned on what you like, look for materials that relate to your project, this maybe any kind of media, book or magazine. Also, see if there is a group of people that have the same or similar vision, get your feet wet; it is a great idea to be with people that want the same things you want. Who knows maybe you can complete the circle and create something new and extraordinary.

Third. Very important: Try to make your personal achievements to be in direct relationship to what enhances your personal life, family life and health. I rather achieve a great relationship with the woman I love than a promotion at work. I have worked now for more than 30 years in the corporate world. I had my achievements, but the rest I have forgotten, do you know what I remember? The good times (and not so good times) with the people I love and the victories we achieved together through many adversities, yes, I remember the many experiences that have enriched my life and the people I have touched and have touched me.

Fourth. Never forget this: Understand

that there are many ways to make money. Not only your job, but the abilities or knowledge you have now can make money. If you ever have ideas and think they can make money, work on them! Regrettably, money ideas have shorter life shelf than milk. I tell you that if you do not do anything about them, they will dissipate and spoil very fast. You have no idea how many people I have met that tell me that such and such thing they just saw in the market, they thought about it many years ago before it was produced. There is nothing worse also, to learn that what you thought could not be done, you find out later someone else did it and is making a lot of dough with that idea!

Fifth. Trust in yourself! Use your common sense always. If you feel you are on the wrong path and/or it has been bothering for a while, then you must probably are. If you think you are being abused cut that and walk away.

Lastly; destroy your fears! Down with all of them! I certify this, from all that I have feared only probably 2 or 3% has ever happened.

But I am going to liberate you today. Have you ever seen any movie where the guy or girl has the gun in his/her hands, but freezes over and cannot shoot the monster/attacker/Zombie? And when you are watching you are almost shouting... Come on! Shoot! But the unfortunate character is paralyzed of fear.

Remember this, Fear will paralyze you!

You will also become a procrastinator always postponing what you need to do, because you do not want to face that problem or circumstance. Let me tell you something, if you are procrastinating something now, that is probably what you should do first. Fear can also make a coward out of any person. Just like people ran away from Goliath because they feared him due to him being a warrior giant, we ran away from our fears because they seem like giants. But they are not undefeatable. Fear can also make people lie. As they fear the punishment: people rather lie than face the correct retribution of his acts.

I guess I can go on an on of the things that fear can induce, but I know you get the point, fear is your enemy and will get you downer and downer until you have no confidence anymore; hence it needs to be eradicated from your life.

Most importantly, listen to me very carefully on this one. Fear is the anti-faith. Not only fear will make you do all the things I just wrote, but also will work against you to bring you the things you exactly fear. Remember Job? The one from the bible? After God allowed the devil to touch his family and then him, this is what he said:

"For the thing which I greatly feared is come upon me, and that which I was afraid of is come unto me" (The book of Job 3:25 KJV)

In the world of eternal principles, he or she who fears will have a negative consequence. Let's take a look to another bible verse:

"There is no fear in love; but perfect love casts out fear, because fear involves torment..."
(1 John 4:118 NKJV)

"Fear involves torment" it is clear that fear, or better said, being or living on fear is by itself a punishment amen of the additional negative things it will bring to your life.

So, as you can see there is negative attraction force that we exercise whether we acknowledge it or not when we live in fear, and interestingly enough, humanity tends to live in fear more than enough than in faith (no wonder why the world is in decline!); we tend to believe more the bad stuff than the good things in life, just like watching the news, see the proportion of bad stories versus good and fulfilling stories? But why do we tend to the negative? Simply because we have been conditioned all our lives to live this way, to react with awe to bad news, we also tend to think and act in the practical and tangible rather than in the realm of the incredible and sublime. We are taught to question ourselves to analyze to be logical and to use whatever means to advance in this life. Life is tough, we are always under pressure to perform, to deliver, to show, to account for all we do and want; or else you are a loser...

But if you change your mind and break away from the things you have learned and start having faith, and even more, you dare to dream and take all the time you can to even shape your plans and projects, believe me, out of the blue little things will start happening that will have no explanation.

Remember that 2 things cannot occupy the same space. Avoid fear and negativism; fill your mind with good possibilities always!

Now here it is my accepted definition of faith which I take from the New Testament from the King James Bible:

"Now faith is the **substance** of the things hoped for, the **evidence** of the things not seen" (Hebrews 11:1 KJV)

Pay close attention here to word "substance". Take a look at the meaning:

> "The tangible matter of which a thing consists; *physical matter* or material:"

Now let's take a look at the word "evidence":

> "That which proves or gives *proof* or disproves something"

Lastly, if we change the Hebrews verse for its meanings it will read like this:

> "Now faith is the *physical matter* of the things hoped for, the *proof* of the things not seen"

"Now faith is the **_physical matter_** of the things hoped for, the **_proof_** of the things not seen"

This verse is unquestionable; literally: WHAT YOU BELIEVE CREATES THE SUTFF YOU WANT AND GIVES PROOF OF THOSE THINGS IN YOUR LIFE!

I have learned a lot from my best friend. But mostly I like the way he goes nonchalant through life. When we first met some years ago, I noticed we had opposite views in what life is concerned. I thought of me that by showing concern and worry it demonstrates my respect and responsibility for my duties, I was educated this way; he on the contrary was always relaxed, but surprisingly came on top always. As an example, he was pulled over by a cop as he was speeding, they let him go; around the same time I got a ticket in a residential zone just for parking wrongly, go figure!

But I always like to learn new things, so I followed his train of thinking and actions; I decided to assimilate his ways, and to my surprise I can certify that his method is better than mine. Now, do not make me wrong, he works hard, but by keeping a positive attitude with people, friends and the environment as well as by trusting all things work for good, things just "happen" for him in the most fortuitous ways, and I am a witness of this!

You see, clearer it cannot be. Whatever you entertain in your mind, that is what your actions will do, and this is how decisively things will happen for you. You do create your life, first in what you believe in your mind, and then in what you act based on those beliefs, then it is done unto you; you attract what you believe and act. The bible is not wrong!

I have noticed as many people as I can, and I have questioned as many people that had made eye contact with me about this. The results are the same: their mind is mostly occupied all day with some worry or concern; "I am late for work, maybe they won't see me slipping by to my office", "my credit card bill was high, what did I buy this time, how will I pay?", "I need to finish my work early so I can pick up my kids on time".

If you do the math, how long do you really think you spend thinking on the things that are positive and good?

I am telling you, for most of the people the time average is so minimal to produce any change. The problem is that is your duty really is to think positively. Look in the next page what the Apostle Paul wrote to the Philippians:

"Finally, brothers and sisters, whatever is true, whatever is noble, whatever is right, whatever is true, whatever is lovely, whatever is admirable –if anything is excellent or praise-worthy **_think_** about such things." (Philippians 4:8 NIV)

Whatever is good you must think on those things; you see in matters if faith, the bible makes a great explanation that you and I can understand and practice, but people rarely follow.

So here is what you must do. Every day if possible take 10 minutes, just meager 10 minutes of your day. You need to re-program yourself. While going to your job, whistle, sing, be happy; think about how you would like things to be, the changes you would like to make and meditate on those things, what small actions can you start doing now. I can assure you that if you do that constantly for one month, out of the blue, things will start happening in your life, You see, once you agree, the universe will start helping you; but you must want it, you must desire it; you must embrace it and rejoice while you do it. Do not worry about doubts that may appear or about your mind wandering in 10,000 other things, remember that discipline and constant effort always win the day. I have done this, and it has worked wonders in my life, but the most important change is that I am happier than ever before, and things come to me and happen out of nowhere!

Today, and specially today, I encourage you to look for you and what benefits you even further than what you been told or have learned, I urge you to take control of your life to purge the normal established conventions and move towards a more natural, happy and healthy life style. Remember the beginning of this book? All things will remain the same unless an external force acts on it. YOU BE THAT FORCE! That, my friend, is your responsibility and no one else's; no one will do that for you! Today I notify you, but it is up to you to take action. And I know you will.

To new beginnings my Captain, cheers!

"It matters not how strait the gate, how charged with punishments the scroll, I am the master of my fate: I am the captain of my soul"
- William Ernest Henley

It has been a pleasure and an honor to share your time with me.

I know you have the power to guide your life and I want you to write me your experiences. Just visit:

www.prometheusgriffing.com

The Captain of your life

"Never in the history of mankind it has been established how to train to become the person we want to be. As we grow up, we are conformed by rules, molds and the environment we interact with, and this, regrettably are the elements that tell us who we are, what we should do and what we should be.

But today, by reading this book, you have decided that all that stops! Because, as you march on your own you will finally be able to decide for yourself and gather the strength and the knowledge to command your ship and captain your life!